SOME TYPES OF PRES

COOKERS

ELECTRIC PRESSURE COOKER

Electric pressure cookers use heat from electricity to heat gas and create pressure. Most electric pressure cookers are equipped with a control panel with an automatic cooking function, which can adjust the time to make it more convenient for users.

Thanks to the effect of heat from the heating plate, the pot heats up, leading to the heat of the pot also increasing, but cannot escape. Thereby, the food in the pot is also cooked faster and softer. Especially without losing the inherent nutrients of the food.

The benefits of using an electric pressure cooker:

Reduce cooking time up to 70%: Users prepare dishes in a short time, especially those that take a lot of time such as heating, steaming, simmering, ...

Save energy up to 50%: Cooking time is fast, so you can save money on electricity every month.

Keep the nutrients inside the food completely: The pot has a sealed design and cannot be opened during the cooking process. Unless you release the pressure in the pot.

Simple control: The electronic control screen is clear, easy to observe and monitor the cooking process and the control functions are clear and easy to understand.

Easy and fast cleaning: The inner pot is equipped with a non-stick coating to help you clean quickly and limit burning, burning and sticking when cooking.

MECHANICAL PRESSURE COOKER

The mechanical pressure cooker is designed with a pot lid with a rubber ring to help keep the lid closed, creating good pressure for the pot. The pot is used to cook on a gas stove, infrared stove, wood stove like other common cooking pots. In addition, there are some mechanical pressure cookers that can be used on induction cookers.

RIB CONGEE

Ingredients

Brown rice 170 gr

Sticky rice 80 gr

Pork Ribs 600 gr

Lean meat 150 gr

Red beans 70 gr

Purple onion 3 pieces

Green onion 2 branches

Cooking oil 1 tablespoon

Common seasoning 1 pinch (salt/sugar/pepper/seasoning)

Implementation tools

Electric pressure cooker, knife, cutting board, meat grinder, spoon,...

How to prepare Rib Porridge with a pressure cooker

1 Prep and marinate ribs

You mix warm water with 1 teaspoon of salt and then put the ribs in, wash and soak for about 5 minutes and then rinse with water. Then you cut the ribs into bite-sized pieces, rinse with salt water again, drain.

Or you can pre-blanch it with boiling water to clean the dirt and remove the bad smell of the ribs.

Marinate ribs with 1 tbsp seasoning, 1/2 tbsp sugar, 1/2 tbsp salt, 1 tsp pepper, 1 tbsp minced shallot. Mix all the ingredients and marinate for 15 minutes for the ribs to absorb the spices.

How to prepare pork ribs clean, not smelly

Squeeze your ribs with salt for about 2-3 minutes and rinse with water.

Using rice vinegar or wine to wash will also remove the smell of ribs.

You can also boil the ribs with boiling water, add a few slices of crushed ginger, then rinse with water.

2 Stir-fry and cook ribs

Turn on the pressure cooker to "Sauté" mode with high heat "More". Next, put in the pot about 1 tablespoon of cooking oil, 1/2 tablespoon of non-fragrant red onion.

Tip: Stir-frying the ribs first will help the fat to be firmer and absorb more seasoning.

Next, you add all the marinated ribs, stir for about 5-7 minutes until the meat is cooked again. Then put about 2.5 liters of warm water into the pot.

You close the lid, do not close the valve and turn on the "Soup" cooking mode with the temperature level of "Normal". Cook for about 10 minutes, then press the "Cancel" button to turn off. Open the lid and skim off the white foam, at the same time check to see if the ribs are cooked, if not, cover the lid and continue cooking for about 5 minutes. If the ribs are cooked, put about 70g of red beans (washed) into the pot.

Finally, cover the pot, close the valve and leave for 5 minutes. You do not need to turn on the pot, but you will use the heat inside the pot to brew red beans and ribs.

3 Minced meat

Put the washed pork in the meat grinder, add 1 tablespoon sugar, 1 tablespoon fish sauce, 1 teaspoon pepper. Close the lid and puree the meat, remember to grind the meat just right to avoid crumbling or too big.

4 Cooking porridge

First, mix 80g of glutinous rice with 170g of brown rice. Then wash the rice mixture with water about 2-3 times, then drain the water, drain.

You open the valve lid and check the bean rib pot to see if the beans are cooked, if not, close the lid, close the valve and cook in the "Soup" mode with the "Normal" temperature level for about 10 minutes to soften the beans.

After the ingredients are cooked, open the lid and put the rice mixture into the pot, close the lid, and close the valve. Turn on the pot to "Porridge" porridge mode with "Normal" level, cook for about 10-15 minutes until the porridge is cooked.

BEEF RICE NOODLES

Ingredients for making Beef Noodles with a pressure cooker

Pork leg 700 gr

Beef encrusted 1.3 kg

Garlic 2 bulbs

Purple onion 1 piece

Cashew oil 2 tablespoons

Fish sauce 2 tablespoons

Fish sauce 2 tablespoons

Cooking oil 3 tablespoons

Common seasoning 1 pinch (salt/sugar/seasoning)

Implementation tools

Pressure cookers, spoons, chopsticks, cups, knives,...

How to cook Beef Noodles in a pressure cooker

1 Prep and sauté the meat

To make beef and pork leg no longer smell, you soak the meat separately with dilute salt water for 10 minutes. Next, you wash it 2-3 times with clean water and let it dry.

Put the pan on the stove, put the beef and pork leg into the pan, put on high heat. You sauté the meat for 5-7 minutes until the meat starts to hunt again, slightly browned on the surface of the meat, then turn off the heat.

Note: You wash the meat thoroughly and soak it in warm water for 5-10 minutes or you can blanch the meat to remove the dirt in the meat. Thus, when cooking the broth will be clearer and more delicious.

2 Meat stew

First, put in a pressure cooker of 2.5 liters of water, close the lid and turn on the "Soup" mode at "More" to heat until the red text turns to "On".

Note: During the process of heating the water in the pot, do not close the valve.

Next, bake the garlic and onions on the stove or bake in the oven (about 180 degrees Celsius) until the onions and garlic are golden. Then, you put the grilled pork leg, onion and garlic into the pressure cooker, add about 1 tablespoon of salt, 1 tablespoon of rock sugar, stir gently and then cover.

Continue to turn on the pot at "Soup" mode with "Less" for about 3 minutes, then open the lid, remove the white foam. Close the lid, lock the valve and continue to stew in "Soup" mode with "Less" level.

Note: When you see the white button on the pot's valve lock pop up, turn off the pot immediately. Because if you cook it for a long time, the pork leg will cook until soft and no longer retain the crunchiness.

After turning off the pot and incubating the pork leg for about 10 minutes, then you unlock the valve and open the lid of the pot, remove the pork leg to a bowl of ice cold water to keep the meat firm. Next, you add the beef, add a little water and smashed lemongrass into the pot. Close the lid and cook with the same "Soup" mode to cook the meat.

During the stew time is 3-5 minutes, you do not lock the valve because you will open the lid to remove the foam. Similar to pork leg stew, after removing, close the lid, lock the valve and continue stewing until the white button is raised.

However, unlike pork leg, after the white button emerges, you do not take it out and continue to stew for about 30 minutes (red button shows L0:33), then turn off the pot.

Trick you:

When adding water to the pot, be careful not to exceed the specified water level in the pot to avoid fire.

In addition, when cooking with "Soup" mode, you can set a timer or set it to 00:00 to cook evenly.

3 Make cashew oil

Put the pot on the stove, put about 3 tablespoons of cooking oil, 2 tablespoons of cashew oil into the pot. Stir until the cashews begin to blacken, the shells crack, then turn off the heat.

Pour the cashew oil mixture through a sieve to extract the oil.

4 Making broth

Using the pot that has made cashew oil, pour about 500ml of water into the pot, add about 2 tablespoons of fish sauce. Stir to dissolve and cook over medium heat until the water in the pot comes to a boil.

After the water in the pot boils, lower the heat to low and let the water mixture settle down, remove the foam. Continue to let the broth settle down again and remove.

5 Cooking broth

You take the meat out of the pressure cooker, put it in a bowl of ice cold water along with the ham legs that have kept the meat firm.

Next, slowly pour the broth into the pot, pour only the clear water, do not remove the residue.

Pour more water into the pot about 2cm from the side of the pot, turn on the button in "Sauté" mode at "More". Do not cover and cook for about 5 minutes, skimming off the top fatsurface.

Add to the pot of broth 2 tablespoons seasoning, 1 tablespoon sugar, 1/2 teaspoon salt, 2 tablespoons fish sauce, stir and cook for about 10 minutes.

Finally, you put about 1-2 tablespoons of cashew oil in the pot (depending on the thickness and lightness of the broth, you can add more cashew oil). Cook for about 5 more minutes and you're done with the broth.

6 Complete

Cut the beef into thin slices to taste, cut the pork leg into pieces and arrange the meat in bowls.

Noodles with hot water for a bowl. Prepare a little more sprouts, water spinach, bananas, onions to serve.

Ladle the broth into the prepared bowls of vermicelli and call the whole family in to enjoy this hot bowl of beef noodle soup right away!

7 Finished Products

Delicious, hot beef noodle soup with all kinds of vegetables. Especially, the tender and cooked meat is interspersed with crispy beef tendons, the pork leg is stewed until the tough skin is dipped with spicy chili fish sauce.

The broth is light and fragrant with the typical Hue fish sauce flavor that makes you crave forever. What's better than enjoying a delicious bowl of beef noodle soup at the weekend?

RICE RISOTTO

Ingredients for making risotto rice

Boiled chicken broth 4 cups

Olive oil 1/4 cup

Onion diced 1 piece

Arborio Rice 2 cups (a delicious Italian rice. If you don't have regular rice, you can also use it)

Saffron 1 teaspoon

Unsalted Butter 50 gr

Thinly grated fresh cheese 1 cup

Implementation tools

mechanical pressure cooker, bowl,...

How to cook risotto rice

1 Sauteed Onions

Put the pressure cooker on the stove, add olive oil, onion and a little salt and stir well. Adjust the stove to the right temperature. Saute for about 3 minutes or until onion is soft.

2 Stir-fry rice

Add the rice to the pot and continue to stir for about 2-3 minutes so that the rice begins to soften.

3 Seasoning

Pour the wine into the pot (pay attention to pour slowly and be careful not to get splashed on the body), then add the saffron, stir until the rice has absorbed all the spices (about 1 minute). Pour the chicken broth into the pot.

4 Cooking rice

Close the lid tightly and place the pot on the stove. Cook for about 6 minutes, adjusting the stove to medium heat.

5 Drain the pressure cooker

After 6 minutes, you open the steam release valve of the pot so that the steam does not stay in the pot, pay attention to avoid burns.

6 Complete

If the rice is too dry, add a little water or chicken broth to the pot, open the lid and cook for 1 more time. You can use a pan to do this step if you find it difficult to do with a pressure cooker.

When the rice is about to run out of water, add butter and grated cheese, stir well and season with spices. Cook until the rice becomes a thick paste, then turn off the heat.

BEEF STEW WITH POTATOES

Materials to prepare:

Beef

Potato

Carrot

Scallion

Coriander

Salt, pepper

How to cook beef stew with potatoes in an electric pressure cooker:

Step 1: Prepare ingredients

Wash the beef, then cut it into small, thick pieces so that when the stew is not crushed, it will be eaten. Potatoes and carrots are peeled, washed, then sliced. Green onions, coriander are picked and washed, cut into pieces to sprinkle over the beef bowl when finished.

Step 2: Cook beef stew with potatoes

Season with pepper, salt and beef to taste. Let it sit for about 20 minutes for the beef to infuse the spices and then stir-fry it for 1 turn. Pour the freshly sautéed beef into the pressure cooker with a little water, then simmer for about 12 minutes.

After 12 minutes, you release the pressure cooker valve quickly to be able to open the pot. Proceed to add the potatoes and carrots, continue to stew for about 3 minutes, then turn off the power to let the steam out of the pot.

Step 3: Enjoy the food

Ladle the beef into a bowl to enjoy, then sprinkle with scallions, coriander and add a little pepper to create aroma for the dish.

BLACK BEAN TEA

Ingredients

Black beans 100 gr

Potato flour 40 gr

Tapioca flour 30 gr

Tapioca powder 2 tablespoons

Coconut milk powder 50 gr

Pandan leaves 50 gr

Vanilla 1 tube

Rock sugar 100 gr

White granulated sugar 200 gr

How to make Black Bean Tea (Black Beans) in a pressure cooker

1 Prepare the ingredients

Wash 100g of black beans, then soak in water overnight for soft beans. Wash pandan leaves, drain.

Pro tip: In order for the tea to not be bitter when cooking, you should pick up all the beans floating on the water during the soaking process.

Next, soak the tapioca starch and tapioca starch for about 30 minutes.

Then, in turn, boil the potato starch and Bang starch separately for 5 minutes, then rinse with cold water several times, drain.

2 Make coconut milk

Mix 50g of coconut milk powder with 250ml of water, then put the mixture in the pot with 50gr of granulated sugar, 50gr of pandan leaves and stir over medium heat until the sugar dissolves, the mixture is warm and hot.

Next, dilute 2 tablespoons of tapioca starch with 3 tablespoons of water in a separate bowl, stirring to dissolve. Then pour this mixture into the pot of coconut milk and continue to stir until the mixture boils, then turn off the heat.

Finally, add 1 more vanilla bean, stir once more and you're done.

Small tip: You can replace 50g of coconut milk powder with 250ml of coconut milk.

3 Cooking tea

Put the soft soaked black beans in the pressure cooker, 1 liter of water, close the lid and turn on the cooking mode for 15 minutes. After 15 minutes, drain the bean incubation valve for another 10 minutes, then take it out into the basket, keeping the bean water in the pot.

Put the pan on the stove, put in the cooked black beans, 150g of granulated sugar, the slugs are peas over low heat for 5-10 minutes to drain, the sugar water is all beans.

Pro tip: This slug makes the beans absorb the sugar water evenly and when cooked, the beans will not be crushed or hard when stored in the refrigerator. However, you must try to bite the pea before the slug, if the bean is soft, then proceed with the slug with sugar.

Put an ordinary pot on the stove, pour in the bean stew, the sugared beans, and continue to cook the tea on medium heat for 5 minutes.

After 5 minutes, add 100g of rock sugar and stir until the sugar dissolves. Next, add in the boiled potato starch and tapioca starch and cook for another 10 minutes.

Finally, put all the coconut milk into the pot, re-season the sweetness to suit the family's taste, then cook for another 5 minutes, then turn off the stove.

Small tip: You can keep the coconut milk separately, if anyone wants to eat it, they can spread it all over.

4 Finished Products

The fragrant black bean tea has the flavor of vanilla and pandan leaves, the thick, sweet, greasy tea blends with the soft black beans, the sweetness permeates each bean.

Besides, you will also feel the chewy, chewy and chewy tapioca flour and chewy dough to create an extremely delicious tea.

BLACK GARLIC

Ingredients

Garlic 500 gr

Beer 330 ml

Implementation tools

Electric pressure cooker (type with Warm mode)

How to cook Make black garlic with a pressure cooker

1 Preliminary processing of ingredients

Peel the thin outermost layer of garlic to avoid dirt, cut the garlic stalk if it is too long.

2 Soak garlic with beer

Garlic, after being preliminarily processed, is poured into the pot, then pour in beer at the ratio of 1 beer can: 1 kg of garlic. Stir well after 5 minutes for the garlic to infuse the beer. After 30 minutes, remove the garlic from the foil and cover well.

3 Cooking garlic

Place the garlic after wrapping the foil in the prepared pressure cooker.

Cover the pot and turn on the heating mode (warm) for 2 consecutive weeks.

4 Finished Products

Garlic naturally ferments and makes garlic more delicious and fragrant. During the incubation process of garlic, you need to keep the pressure cooker in a cool place, avoiding direct sunlight on the pot.

BEEF NOODLE SOUP

Ingredients for making beef noodle soup with pressure cooker

Beef bone 2.5 kg (tub bone or tail bone)

Beef neck bone 1.5 kg

Cooked meat 1 kg (with beef)

Beef balls and rare meat served if you like some

Fresh noodle soup 2 kg

Pho seasoning 2 packs (small pack)

Dried Pho seasoning 1 pack (43g including cinnamon/anise and some other nuts)

Sugar rock 50 gr

Chicken soup powder 3 tbsp

Ginger 170 gr (1 medium)

Onion 2 pieces

Pepper 3 teaspoons

Scallion head / onion leaves / coriander 1 little

Herbs served with Pho 1 little

1 pinch salt/seasoning

How to choose to buy fresh beef bones

You should buy bone marrow or oxtail bones will make the broth sweeter and tastier than other bones.

Choose to buy fresh, red bones that feel heavy in the hand. Avoid buying frozen bones of unknown origin to protect health.

Do not buy beef bones that have a fresh white or pale color, and feel light when you hold them because they are old bones when cooking the broth is not good, easy to smell.

How to choose to buy fresh beef

Fresh beef will have a dark red color, the meat is evenly colored, the cut surface of the meat is shiny. The piece of meat when smelled has a characteristic fresh meat smell, no strange smell.

Should choose meat when touching feels dry film, no sticky feeling. Try pressing on the meat, if it is fresh, it will have elasticity, when pressed, it will not be concave.

Do not buy meat when you feel your hands are marinated because it is soaked beef. With pho, you should choose beef fillet or beef when eating, it will be softer and sweeter.

Implementation tools

Multi-function pressure cooker, knife, spoon, bowl, cutting board,...

How to cook Beef Pho with a pressure cooker

1 Preliminary preparation of bones and beef

Beef bones, beef after washing, take it to soak with salt and vinegar for about 5 minutes, then rinse with clean water and bring to a boil.

Put bones and meat in a pot, add 1 liter of water, 1 teaspoon of salt, cover and bring to a boil. Boil the bones and meat for about 5-7 minutes, then take them out and wash them under the tap again to make them clean.

2 Grilled onions and ginger

Peel 2 onions and put them on the stove with 1/2 ginger. For fragrant ripe onions and ginger, scrape off the burnt black outer skin, take it out and wash it.

3 Bone Cellars

Put the pre-prepared beef bones (do not add the neck bones) to the pressure cooker, fill the bones with water (about 2/3 of the pot), add 1 teaspoon of pepper and 1 tablespoon of salt to the pot.

Close the lid, lock the valve and press the "Manual" button to adjust the stewing time for 60 minutes. After stewing the bones for about 6-8 hours for the beef bones to come out of all the fresh water.

Strain the broth through a sieve to get the clear water. After filtering the broth, you separate all the meat and tendons around the beef bones, set aside and bring the bones to stew for the second time.

Put the beef bones and tendons in the pot, add the neck bones and cooked meat, fill the pressure cooker 2/3 with water, add 1 teaspoon pepper, 1 tablespoon seasoning and stew for 30 minutes. old degree. After cooking, let it rest for another 30 minutes.

Continue to filter the broth through the second sieve, remove the fat from the broth to reduce boredom.

4 Cooking broth

In the pho flavor pack, take out the cinnamon, anise, and cardamom and roast in a pan with low heat until fragrant, then add the remaining ingredients to roast for another 3 minutes, then turn off the heat. Put in a filter bag to cook the broth later.

Put the broth into a large pot, add cold water to make 12 liters of water, then remove the bones (the bones have been filtered and the tendons), onions and grilled ginger, the head of green onions, and bring the broth to a boil.

To make the water richer, add 3 tablespoons of chicken soup powder, 1 teaspoon of pepper, 2 packets of pho seasoning, a bag of roasted cinnamon and cook for 80-90 minutes on medium heat.

Before turning off the stove, you taste it again to suit your family's taste and add beef balls if you like.

5 Complete

While the broth is cooking, prepare some new ingredients for the pho.

The top part of the onion is trimmed with flowers to decorate it beautifully, and the leaves are cut finely with a little cilantro, cut into bite-sized pieces of beef. You can also cut more fresh beef to make rare meat to eat with.

Prepare a pot of sauce and put fresh pho noodles in for about 5 seconds, then take them out.

Put pho noodles in a bowl with bean sprouts ready, add beef, beef tendon, rare meat, pour broth on top, add cilantro to make it fragrant and beautiful.

RED BEAN TEA WITH COCONUT WATER

Ingredients

Red beans 250 g

Sugar 250 g

Salt 1 teaspoon

100 ml coconut milk (canned type sold in supermarkets)

Implementation tools

Pressure cooker, cup, spoon,...

How to make red bean soup with coconut water in a pressure cooker

1 Bean stew

Soak red beans in water for 8 hours.

When the time is up, take out the beans, rinse, and drain.

Put the beans in the pot, then, cover the beans with water, about 800ml.

2 Cooking tea

Add 1 teaspoon of salt to the pressure cooker, select the bean cooking mode (cook for 30 minutes). After 30 minutes, open the pot lid, add 250g sugar, stir well. Select the nutritious cooking mode and cook the beans for another 30 minutes.

3 Finished Products

When the tea is cooked, you scoop it out into a cup and add coconut milk to make the tea more delicious.

BEEF TENDON STEW WITH LEMONGRASS

Ingredients

Beef tendon 300 gr

1 piece white radish

Lemongrass 4 branches (smashed)

Coconut 1 fruit (get water)

Basil / scallions 1 little

Cooking oil 2 tablespoons

1 pinch salt

How to cook beef tendon with lemongrass

1 Preliminary processing of beef tendons

Bought beef tendons are washed and deodorized by soaking them in dilute salt water for 2-3 minutes, then removed, drained and cut into squares with a thickness of 1 knuckle.

To reduce the smell of beef tendon, you put the crushed lemongrass in the marinade.

Ways to deodorize beef tendons

Method 1: Rub beef tendon with a little salt for about 5 minutes, then rinse with water, then cut into small pieces.

Method 2: Use a little white wine to squeeze the beef tendon for about 5 minutes and then wash it with water.

Method 3: Use 1 branch of ginger to smash, rub it on the beef tendon and then wash it with water.

2 Preliminary preparation of other ingredients

White radish washed, peeled and cut into bite-sized pieces.

Basil picks up leaves and young tops, washes and dries.
Onions cut into bite-sized pieces.

3 Beef tendon stew

Put a pot on the stove and add 2 tablespoons of cooking oil. Add finely chopped scallions to the pan.

After that, you add beef tendons and stir-fry until cooked, then put in the water of 1 coconut and bring to a boil.

When the pot of beef tendon is boiling, add the radishes with 2 teaspoons of salt and cook until soft. Stew beef tendon for about 45 - 50 minutes with low heat until beef tendon is soft.

After the beef tendon is cooked, season to taste, then turn off the heat and scoop out into a bowl, garnish with a little basil on top.

Outward remittance:

To avoid crushing the radish during the cooking process, you should take the radish out after the stew is soft and then continue to stew the beef tendon.

The way to test the ripeness of the radish is very simple, you use a chopstick or a sharp stick to pierce the radish, if the chopsticks go through easily, the radish is cooked soft.

In addition, you can also shorten the time of stewing beef tendons by using a pressure cooker to cook.

4 Finished Products

Delicious fresh beef tendon is stewed extremely soft, extremely delicious mixed with sweet broth, is a delicious and attractive dish for family meals.

SOY SAUCE STEW RIBS

Ingredients

Ribs 1 kg

Red onion 4 bulbs (choose the big one)

Garlic 2 bulbs

Green onion 6 branches

Cooking oil 2 tablespoons

Soy sauce 2 tablespoons

Common seasoning 1 pinch

(salt/seasoning/pepper/monosodium glutamate/sugar)

Implementation tools

Pressure cooker, knife, cup, spoon, bowl,...

How to make Soy Sauce Stew Ribs

1 Prepare other ingredients

Onions and garlic are peeled, washed and chopped.

Scallions remove damaged leaves, wash and cut into small pieces.

2 Prepare and marinate beef ribs

Purchased beef ribs are washed with dilute salt water and then rinsed with cold water.

Marinate beef ribs with minced garlic and shallot, 1 pinch of pepper, 1/2 teaspoon of salt, 1/2 teaspoon of MSG, 2 tablespoons of cooking oil.

Add 2 tablespoons of soy sauce, 4 tablespoons of filtered water and 3 teaspoons of sugar, stir well, then pour into the ribs and mix until the spices are absorbed into the ribs. Marinate ribs for 15 minutes.

3 Beef rib stew

Put the marinated ribs in the pressure cooker, turn on the soup mode and stew the ribs for 20 minutes.

After 20 minutes, open the lid and turn the ribs to absorb the spices, then stew for another 30 minutes and it's done.

4 Finished Products

Stewed ribs in soy sauce are rich in flavor, fragrant, and tender ribs are soaked in spices. The dish can be eaten with rice or vermicelli.

GREEN PEPPER STEW BEEF TAIL

Ingredients

Beef tail 1 kg

Carrots 2 pieces

Potatoes 3 pieces

Green pepper 30 gr

1/2 cup ginger

Coriander 3 branches

Purple onion 3 pieces

Minced garlic 2 tablespoons

White wine 10 ml

Cooking oil 2 tablespoons

Implementation tools

Pressure cooker, pot, knife, bowl, cutting board,...

How to cook Stewed Beef Tail with Green Pepper

1 Preliminary processing of ox tail

Buy the cow's tail to shave off the remaining hair. Then wash the ox tail with alcohol, use crushed ginger to rub the outside so that the ox tail no longer has a bad smell, remove dirt.

Next, boil the ox tail in boiling water for about 2-3 minutes, until the meat is slightly firm and cut into bite-sized pieces.

2 Preliminary preparation of other ingredients

Potatoes and carrots washed and peeled. Use a knife to cut carrots into small pieces, and potatoes to cut into bite-sized pieces.

Peel the red onion and cut it into quarters (cut into areca segments).

Green pepper washed, drained.

3 Stir-fry beef tail

You take the pressure cooker on the stove, put a little oil in the pot. Add about 2 tablespoons minced garlic, saute garlic over medium heat.

Then, you put all the ox tail into the pot, stir well. Stir-fry the oxtails for about 10 minutes so that the oxtails absorb the flavor of the fried garlic.

4 Beef tail stew with green pepper and vegetables

First, you pour water to cover the ox tail first, heat it on medium heat. When the water in the pot starts to boil, remove the white foam. You add about 500 - 700ml of water to the pot, stir well. Cover and simmer the oxtail for 30 minutes.

After 30 minutes, you open the lid, put the potatoes and carrots in the pot, stir well and then cover the stew for another 10 minutes.

Next, you just put all the purple onion and green pepper in the pot, stir well. Add a little more seasoning to your taste.

Finally, close the lid and stew for about 10 more minutes and you are done with the dish.

5 Finished Products

The stewed oxtail is presented in a bowl, hot, fragrant, spreading the smell throughout your kitchen.

Sweet broth from vegetables and oxtail. Beef tail with soft meat, tough skin, when you eat you will feel the crunchy inside. The stewed potatoes and carrots were moderately tender, not mushy. Green pepper adds a bit of pungent flavor to the dish.

GREEN PEPPER STEW STOMACH

Ingredients

Pork stomach 700 gr

Green pepper 200 gr

100 gr . white radish

Fresh coconut 200 ml

Purple onion 20 gr

Vinegar 20 ml

Salt 10 gr

Seasoning powder 10 gr

Cooking oil 50 ml

Spinach 200 gr

Fresh vermicelli 200 gr

Ingredients for stewed stomach dishes with green pepper

Implementation tools

Pressure cooker, stove, grill,...

How to cook Green Pepper Stew Stomach

1 Preliminary processing of ingredients

First, wash your stomach with a little white vinegar and salt and then rinse it with cold water. Then grill the stomach on the gas stove for the two sides of the stomach to dry slightly. This step will help the stomach to be crispy, fragrant and clean of all odors and viscous.

After baking, you wash again with cold water and then cut the stomach into bite-sized pieces.

Wash green pepper, wash radish and cut into bite-sized pieces, chopped red onion.

Stomach after chopped, marinated with 1 teaspoon of seasoning seeds, 1/2 amount of green pepper, leave for about 15 minutes to absorb the seasoning.

Tip: Washing the stomach with a little salt and vinegar will help deodorize the stomach.

2 Stomach cellars

Put the pressure cooker on the stove, add a little cooking oil, hot oil for the purple onion, then add the stomach and stir for about 2 minutes. Avoid stir-frying the stomach for too long, the stomach will be tough and not delicious anymore.

Then you add coconut water, add a little water to cover the stomach with water, add green pepper and radish, cover the pressure cooker and stew for about 15-20 minutes.

After the stew is finished, season to taste and then you scoop it out into a small pot and serve it with delicious vermicelli and spinach.

Note: Using a pressure cooker to stew the stomach will be softer and more delicious.

3 Finished Products

Green pepper is very good for health, has the effect of preventing colds, warming the stomach, stimulating digestion, which is very suitable when used in erratic rainy and windy days like this.

FROZEN PORK LEG

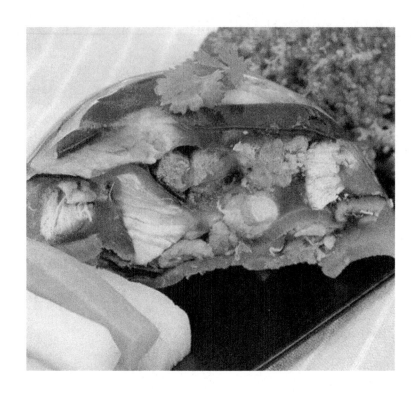

Ingredients

Pork leg meat 500 gr

Pork skin 200 gr

Onion 1 piece

Purple onion 3 pieces

Shiitake mushrooms 50 gr (soaked)

Black fungus / wood ear mushrooms 50 gr (soaked)

1 little cooking oil

Fish sauce 1 teaspoon

1 pinch salt/seasoning

Implementation tools

Electric pressure cooker (or gas pressure cooker), pan, knife, cutting board, spoon,...

How to cook frozen pork leg

1 Prepare and marinate pork leg meat

To get rid of the bad smell, buy the pig's feet with a razor to shave off the hair, then rub with salt, then rinse with clean water. Cut pork leg into medium pieces and remove fat and bones.

Marinate pork leg with 1/2 teaspoon of salt, 1 teaspoon of seasoning, 1 teaspoon of fish sauce for 30 minutes to infuse the meat with spices.

2 Preliminary processing of pig skin

First, you soak the pork skin in diluted salt water for about 15 minutes, then wash it 2-3 times with clean water and cut it into bite-sized pieces.

Put a pot of water on the stove, add a little salt, when the water boils, put the pork skin in, blanch for about 2 minutes, then take it out, put it in a bowl of cold water to keep the skin crispy and not brown, then put it in a basket and let it dry. .

How to properly and cleanly prepare pig skin

You can clean the hair by dipping the pig's skin in boiling water for about 3 minutes to tighten the skin, then pull out all the hairs left on the knife with tweezers.

Use a knife to filter out all the excess fat under the skin to make the skin more crispy.
Wash lemon and salt to help white and clean pig skin.

3 Stir-fry meat
Put a little oil in the pan and fry it with 1 minced purple onion.

Next, you put the bowl of marinated meat into the non-oiled pan and continue to stir until the meat starts to hunt again, then turn off the heat.

4 Cook pork leg meat

Put the meat in the pressure cooker, pour 1 liter of water to cover the meat, then cook for 5 minutes.

At the end of the cooking time, the pot switches to warming mode, release the pressure in the pot.

5 Cook pork skin, onion

Open the lid of the pressure cooker, add the pork skin and onion and cook with the meat for 15 minutes.

After cooking, drain the pressure as usual and remove the pork skin and onion.

6 Complete

Shiitake and shiitake mushrooms soak in water until they bloom, then cut them into fibers and put them in the pot, sprinkle with pepper and stir well, cook for another 5 minutes.

When the cooking time is up, you release the pressure, when the meat is tender, you scoop it out into a bowl, let it cool, and put it in the fridge for 4 hours for the meat to freeze.

7 Finished Products

Delicious soft frozen meat, fatty leopard with wood ear, crunchy shiitake mushrooms are extremely attractive. This is a familiar dish, indispensable in the holidays.

Frozen meat dipped in fish sauce, add a little sauerkraut, salted tubers to eat with hot rice, there's nothing better, right! Let's make the dish, hope you enjoy it.

STEAMED PATE

Ingredients

Pork liver 350 gr

Lean pork mince 500 gr

Fat pieces 350 gr

Bread 2 pieces

Fresh milk without sugar 340 ml

100 gr . unsalted butter

Onion 1 piece

Purple onion 2 pieces

Garlic 3 cloves

Cooking oil 2 tablespoons

Common seasoning 1 little (sugar/salt/seasoning/ground pepper)

Implementation tools

Pressure cooker, meat grinder, spoon, bowl, brass, cutting board, 18cm diameter round pate mold,...

How to cook Steamed Pate with a pressure cooker

1 Preliminary processing of liver, meat, pork fat

First, with 350g of purchased pork liver, you wash it with water, drain it, then cut it into large pieces with a thickness of about 1cm, put everything in a bowl and pour in about 170ml of unsweetened fresh milk, soak for 30 minutes. .

With 500g of minced meat, you also wash it with water and drain. Then, from the large block of meat, you cut 7 pieces of meat in advance, the big one to line the mold, the rest of the meat you cut into many small pieces.

For 350g of fat, wash and dry. Bring a pot of water to a boil with high heat and then put the fat in the pot, until the water boils, use a spoon to skim off the floating foam.

Take 1/3 of a piece of fat and cut it into large pieces to line the mold similar to the meat. The rest cut into several small pieces.

2 Preliminary preparation of other ingredients
Tear 2 pieces of bread into the bowl, pour 170ml of fresh milk evenly throughout the bowl so that the bread samples are soaked in milk.

Take 1 onion, peel off the skin, root, wash with water, drain and cut into dices.

With 2 purple onions, 3 garlic cloves, peel, wash, drain and mince finely.

3 Place fat and meat in the bottom of the pan

Prepare a round mold with a diameter of 18cm, first place the large pieces of grease that have been cut into the first layer on the bottom of the mold. Next, you arrange 7 large pieces of minced meat in a layer on top.

4 Puree and stir-fry the pate . mixture

Heat a pan on the stove over medium heat, add 2 tablespoons of cooking oil, wait until the oil is hot, then add all the diced onions, red onions and minced garlic and saute until fragrant.

Continue, you put all the pork liver, minced lean meat, the remaining fat with the onion, garlic, and bread soaked in milk into the meat grinder and puree it.

Put the pureed mixture into a large bowl, marinate in 1 teaspoon of salt, 1 teaspoon of ground pepper, 2 teaspoons of seasoning, 1/2 tablespoon of sugar and mix well.

Put a pan on the stove and heat it on medium heat, add the marinated pureed pate mixture and stir-fry until cooked, while stirring, remember to stir constantly so as not to burn!

5 Molding

Next, you put the freshly fried pate mixture into the mold lined with two layers of fat and meat, then use a spatula to spread the pate mixture evenly and then spread it evenly so that the upper part of the pate is flat.

At this time, cut 100g of unsalted butter into 4 equal pieces and arrange on top of the pate.

6 Steamed pate

Put the pressure cooker on the stove, Place on a clean towel folded in quarters, cover with water.

Next, you put the mold containing the pate mixture in, cook on high heat until the water in the pot boils, then lower the heat to very low, then close the lid and screw the lid tightly to boil under pressure for about 1 hour.

Tip: If using an electric pressure cooker, you also put the pate mold in the same pot as above and select the "Cook" or "Stew" function and set the time for about 1 hour!

Then, you take out the cooked pate, let the pate cool completely, then cover with cling film, place in the refrigerator to cool for 2 hours.

Finally, you take out the pate, remove the food wrap, put the pate on a plate and enjoy!

7 Finished Products

With steaming with pate with a rice cooker, the finished product is still sticky and sticky without being crushed. Especially, the pate is of the same quality as the famous pate box sold in the market.

You cut a little pate and then fill the bread with a little chili sauce and enjoy this delicious taste right away!

IMITATION DUCK

Ingredients

1/2 duck (about 500g)

Fresh bamboo shoots 1 kg

Lemongrass 6 branches

Choke 1 left

4 chili peppers

Minced garlic 2 tablespoons

Minced purple ham 1 tbsp

Sauce 4 tbsp

Roasted peanuts 1 tbsp

Oil curry 1 tbsp

Fish sauce 2 tablespoons

Five flavors 1/2 pack (about 1 teaspoon)

Common seasoning 1 little (salt/sugar/monosodium glutamate/seasoning)

Implementation tools

Pressure cooker, torch, pot, fork, spoon,...

How to cook civet duck with a pressure cooker

1 Prepare and marinate duck meat

Buy duck meat, wash it. Use a torch to toast or lightly roast duck. Then cut the duck into bite-sized pieces and wash again with clean water, drain.

How to prepare duck without smell

Method 1: Use white wine and crushed ginger to rub evenly on the duck for a few minutes, then rinse with water.

Method 2: Use salt to rub evenly on the duck, then use a halved lemon to rub it on the duck again and rinse with water.
See details: How to choose, buy and prepare fresh, delicious duck meat without any odors

2 Boil bamboo shoots and make dipping sauce
Wash your bamboo shoots, then cut them into bite-sized pieces.

To remove toxins in bamboo shoots, you boil bamboo shoots through a lot of water until the water in which the bamboo shoots are boiled is no longer yellow, then take them out and drain.

Tips to effectively eliminate toxins in bamboo shoots
To remove all the toxins in bamboo shoots, in addition to the above method, you can soak bamboo shoots in water to wash rice for 2 days, then wash and process dishes.

You can boil it with about 1 handful of spinach leaves, then take out and drain.

Besides, soaking bamboo shoots overnight with filtered water, changing the water every 2 hours is also a way to help eliminate toxins.

To make the dipping sauce, add 2 tablespoons of soy sauce, 1 branch of minced lemongrass, 4 minced chili peppers, then squeeze 1 kumquat, then mix well, finally add 1 tablespoon of roasted peanuts to complete.

3 Cooking civet duck

Prepare a pressure cooker, add marinated duck meat and pre-prepared bamboo shoots, add 1.5 liters of water. Cover pot and cook for 20 minutes.

After 20 minutes, leave the lid on the duck meat incubator for another 10 minutes, then drain the valve.

Finally, put the fake civet duck meat from the pressure cooker into a regular pot, season to taste according to your taste, continue to boil for about 5 minutes and then turn off the stove.

Outward remittance:

Pressure cooker helps Duck stew is quick and soft, saving cooking time compared to stewing in a normal pot.

During the pressure cooker stew process, you must not open the lid to taste or inspect the meat. Should stew for enough time, incubate for at least 5 minutes and then drain the valve.

The seasoning or adding cilantro, you should put it in a regular pot and then increase or decrease the seasoning later!

4 Finished Products

The fake civet duck cooked in a pressure cooker has been completed, the strong aroma of lemongrass and spices is very attractive. The tender duck meat is just cooked to perfection, combined with delicious crispy bamboo shoots, delicious duck juice, evenly absorbed into the seasoning.

This dish is very delicious with fresh vermicelli, bread or hot rice!

CHICKEN WITH TRADITIONAL MEDICINE

Prepare materials:

Chicken or evil chicken: 1 chicken

Traditional medicine: 1 bag

1 handful of wormwood leaves

Spices: soup powder, fish sauce, turmeric powder, seasoning powder, pepper,…

Making:

After pre-processing, clean the chicken, marinate the chicken with a little seasoning powder and turmeric powder until golden and then insert the wormwood in the middle of the chicken body.

Continue, you spread a layer of wormwood and herbal medicine to the bottom of the pot and then put the chicken on top

Add water to cover the chicken body, then cover the electric pressure cooker and stew for about 10 minutes, you have a nutritious traditional Chinese medicine chicken.

After cooking, the dish has the rich flavor of traditional Chinese medicine, the sweetness of chicken and the characteristic dark brown of wormwood leaves.

PORK LEG STEWED WITH LOTUS SEEDS

Ingredients:

1 boneless pork leg (it's better to use the front leg)

Lotus seeds

Carrot

Mushrooms, Onion

The smell of ships

Making:

The legs are shaved, then marinated with seasoning seeds, spices, chopped dried onions and then stored in the refrigerator for about 2 hours to infuse the spices.

Lotus seeds, soaked shiitake mushrooms. Simmer on low heat so that the lotus seeds are ripe but still not crushed, set aside.

Pour the ginseng broth over the meat and simmer in a pressure cooker for about 20 minutes. Use chopsticks to test to see if the meat is tender, if the meat is not tender, then cook again until the meat is tender. If you can skewer the chopsticks easily, pour the lotus seeds and shiitake mushrooms into the pot to cook, seasoning to taste.

Onions are cut into areca, carrots are cut into thin slices, chopped coriander onions are waiting for the meat to be prepared, then pour into the pot.

This dish is very suitable in winter and eat with rice or bread. Each fiber is ripe, soft, fragrant, and boneless. Eating both skin and fat does not feel greasy, but on the contrary, it is very attractive from the elderly to young children.

BAKED RIBS

Material

1 kg whole ribs

2 Siamese coconuts

Garlic + onion + minced red onion

1 large cup of tomato sauce + 3 teaspoons of sugar + 4 teaspoons of vinegar + 1 teaspoon of oyster sauce + 2 teaspoons of pepper + 1 teaspoon of soy sauce + 1/2 cup of water + paprika or chili sauce if you want it spicy

Steps

Prepare ribs.

Cook with 2 Siamese coconuts and 1 pinch of salt. 50 minutes slowcook.

Prepare materials

1. Onion + garlic + minced onion.
2. 1 large cup ketchup + 3 teaspoons sugar + 4 teaspoons vinegar + 1 teaspoon oyster sauce + 2 teaspoons pepper + 1 teaspoon soy sauce + 1/2 cup water + paprika or chili sauce if you want spicy

Sauteed the golden onion. Add the above mixture to the bowl and stir, on medium heat until thickened.

Ribs cooked

Put the ribs in the mixture and cover them evenly and bring to the grill.

COOKED PORK CHOPS

Material:

1 pork roll, choose the first one will be better

Batch, shrimp paste, purple onion, galangal, lemongrass, turmeric powder, spring onion, seasoning seeds, monosodium glutamate, sugar, ...

Perform:

Galangal washed thoroughly then sliced thinly or brought and then crushed. Red onion peeled, washed and chopped.

Pork rolls are washed with salt water, then cut into bite-sized pieces. Marinate spring rolls with galangal, turmeric powder and some onions, batches, shrimp paste, seasoning seeds. Place the pork chops in the refrigerator for a few hours to infuse the flavors.

Take a pot and put cooking oil in, add onions and fry until fragrant. Next, put the hock in and cook until the meat is tender, skip the electric pressure cooker and add water and cook for 30 minutes until soft.

Then check to see, if the meat is not tender, you can continue to cook until it is cooked, you can re-season to taste. Put the fake civet in a bowl, eat it with rice or vermicelli, it's very delicious.

SALAD POTATO

Material

6 potatoes, medium size, washed

250ml water

¼ onion, sliced lengthwise

1 stalk of celery, cut into pieces

Salt, pepper

3 hard-boiled eggs, sliced

1 tablespoon finely chopped dill

125ml mayonnaise

1 teaspoon yellow mustard

1 teaspoon apple cider vinegar

Necessary tools

Because potatoes are an ingredient that takes a long time to cook, a pressure cooker will help you shorten a lot of time when preparing this delicious salad.

In addition, the pressure cooker is also especially suitable when it comes to cooking stews such as beans, tendons, etc. in a very short time. If there is no electronic pressure cooker, a mechanical pressure cooker is also a very good choice for housewives.

How to make potato salad in a pressure cooker

How to do it

Put the water and potatoes in the pressure cooker. Cook on high pressure for 3 minutes. After the time is up, wait for another 3 minutes for the pressure in the pot to completely dissipate.

Once the pressure in the pot is gone, open the lid, remove the potatoes, let cool, peel and cut into squares.

To alternate layers of potatoes, onion and celery in large bowl. Sprinkle salt and pepper on each layer. Top sprinkled with dill.

Place mayonnaise, mustard, and apple cider vinegar in a bowl, mix well. Pour this sauce mixture over the potatoes. Refrigerate for at least an hour before using.

3. Finished Product

Store in the fridge and serve whenever you like. Place a few slices of sliced egg on top for extra flavor.

STUFFED BITTER MELON

Materials to prepare:

Bitter gourd (bitter gourd)

Minced meat

Live rolls

Wood ear (cat's ear mushroom), shiitake mushroom

Fresh onions, dried onions

Seasoning (sugar, salt, pepper)

How to cook stuffed bitter melon with an electric pressure cooker:

Step 1: Prepare ingredients
Wash the bitter melon, cut it in half, scrape the intestines with a spoon. Soak in water for 10-15 minutes with cold water to reduce bitterness, then take out and drain.

For shiitake and wood ear mushrooms, soak them in hot water, wash them until they bloom, and then cut them into small pieces. Peel the dried onions, smash to mix with minced meat. The green onions are cut into small pieces to sprinkle on the bowl when the dish is done.

Step 2: Marinate seasoning and stuffing with meat
Prepare a large bowl for the meat, add the raw pork to marinate the spices. Season to taste (salt, cooking oil, pepper, dried onions) to taste and then mix well to infuse the meat with the spices.

Then, use a spoon to scoop up a sufficient amount of filling to slowly enter the bitter gourd's intestines, gently pressing the filling tightly.

Step 3: Cook bitter melon

Pour a sufficient amount of water into the pressure cooker, open the lid, when the water boils, add bitter melon stuffed with meat, add a little seasoning to the pot of water. Close the lid of the pot, stew for about 10 minutes, then take it out, or if you like to eat more, stew more.

Step 4: Enjoy
Ladle bitter melon soup into a bowl, sprinkle with fresh onions and enjoy.

BRAISED BEEF

Ingredients for Braised Beef

Beef ribs 1 kg

Beef tendon 1 kg

Lemongrass 10 plants

3 carrots

Potatoes 3 pieces

Purple onion 3 pieces

Garlic 4 cloves

Ginger 1 branch

Fresh coconut water 500 ml

Beef broth 1 pack (50g)

Braised beef seasoning 1 pack (50g)

1 little white wine

Common seasoning 1 little (sugar / salt / seasoning powder / monosodium glutamate)

Implementation tools

Pressure cookers, spoons, chopsticks, cups, plates,...

How to cook Braised Beef with a pressure cooker

1 Prepare the ingredients

To clean and deodorize beef, soak the beef ribs and tendons in dilute salt water for about 5 minutes, then rub it with white wine for about 10 minutes and then rinse with water several times.

Lemongrass you peel off the layer of dry leaves, withering worms outside, wash, smash the lemongrass root and then cut into pieces about 1 finger long. Red onion, ginger, garlic remove the root, peel and wash, smash then mince.

Carrots, potatoes, peeled, washed, cut into bite-sized pieces.

How to prepare clean, odorless beef

You can use salt to rub the meat evenly and then wash it with water.

Soak the meat with a little diluted white wine for about 5 minutes and then rinse with water.

In addition, you can also use lemon to rub the meat and then wash it with water.

2 Marinated beef

After cleaning beef ribs and beef tendon, put in a marinade bowl with 5 tablespoons of sugar, 5 tablespoons of seasoning powder, 1 tablespoon of salt, 1 teaspoon of MSG and add all the onions, garlic, and minced ginger. Puree, mix well to infuse the seasoning into the meat.

Then you put in the beef marinade bowl 1 pack of braised beef seasoning powder and 1 pack of braised beef broth, mix well to marinate the beef evenly on the beef. Cover the bowl with cling film and put it in the fridge.

Pro tip: Beef is best when marinated overnight, if you don't have time, you should marinate the beef at least 1 hour before cooking!

3 Cook braised beef

You take the pressure cooker on the stove, put the marinated beef and lemongrass cut into pieces and mix well.Put in 500ml pot of fresh coconut water, cover and simmer beef for 30 minutes.

After 30 minutes, open the lid, add the potatoes and carrots, stir well, then cover and simmer for another 10 minutes.

After 10 minutes, open the lid, use the tip of the chopsticks to skewer the potatoes, the carrots are soft, taste the seasoning for the last time to taste and then turn off the stove.

Braised beef is ready to serve and enjoy!

4 Finished Products

Braised beef is presented with eye-catching colors, the smooth broth spreads the aroma throughout your family's kitchen.

Beef ribs are simmered, soft and delicious. The beef tendon is tender, crispy and still retains its attractive crispiness. Carrots and potatoes are soft and fragrant, making the dish even more attractive.

Braised beef is suitable for serving with vermicelli, bread or hot white rice, which are very delicious and catchy. This will definitely be the perfect choice for the weekend menu for you to treat your whole family!

BRAISED MEAT

Ingredients

Bacon 500 gr (bacon)

Fresh coconut water 200 ml

Duck eggs 6 eggs

Minced garlic 1 tablespoon

Minced red onion 2 tablespoons

3 chili peppers

Wine 1 tbsp

Fish sauce 2 tablespoons

Common seasoning 1 little (Salt/sugar/seasoning/pepper)

How to cook braised pork with a pressure cooker

1 Preliminary processing of ingredients

To clean meat, when you buy it, use 1 tablespoon of salt to rub, then wash with clean water, cut into bite-sized pieces about 1 finger.

How to remove the smell of pork

Before processing, blanch the pork in boiling water for about 3 minutes with 1 crushed purple onion, onion will help eliminate odors very well.

In addition, you can also add a little white wine to the meat broth before taking out the meat because white wine will help remove the odor in the meat most effectively.

After that, wash the meat with cold water and then carry it for further processing, the meat will no longer have a bad smell and the dish made from pork will be more delicious.

2 Marinate meat

For better taste and color, marinate the meat with 2 tablespoons of sugar for 30 minutes.

Then you marinate with 2 tablespoons of seasoning, 2 teaspoons of pepper, 1 tablespoon of wine, 2 tablespoons of fish sauce, 1 tablespoon of minced garlic, 2 tablespoons of minced purple onion.

Mix well and marinate for another 30 minutes for the meat to absorb the spices.

Note: If you have time, you can also marinate the meat in the refrigerator overnight to make the meat more delicious!

3 Boil duck eggs

Wash duck eggs, put in a pot and boil for 5-7 minutes on medium heat. Then let it cool and peel it off.

How to boil peeled duck eggs quickly:

Put eggs in a pot, cover with water and add a little vinegar to make it easier to peel.

After boiling the eggs for about 7 minutes, take them out and put them in a bowl of cold water and peel them, this will make the eggs cool quickly and the eggshells will easily peel off, convenient for peeling.

4 Meat Warehouse

You plug in the pressure cooker to adjust the time for 5 minutes, add 2 tablespoons of sugar, 2 tablespoons of filtered water, stir with chopsticks until the sugar water turns brown.

Next, put the marinated meat into the pot and stir-fry again, add 200ml of fresh coconut water and filtered water to cover the meat, cover and adjust the stock for 10 minutes.

After 10 minutes, you release the pressure, add duck eggs, 3 chili peppers, re-season to taste, continue to adjust the time for another 10 minutes to complete.

Note: When releasing the pressure steam, be careful not to get burned by the heat.
You can also use an earthenware pot instead of a pressure cooker!

5 Finished Products
The delicious Chinese braised pork belly is ready and can be served hot. The dish is soft, delicious, rich, fatty leopard meat combined with extremely delicious duck eggs to bring rice!

TRIPE BRAISED

Ingredients

1 piece ginger

Beef intestine 1.5 kg

Vinegar 130 ml

Baking soda powder 1 tbsp

Onion 1 piece

Anise flowers 3 pieces

White wine 1 tbsp

Garlic 6 cloves

Purple onion 1 piece

Five-spice powder 1 teaspoon

Soy sauce 3 tbsp

1 piece dry chili

1 little fresh chili

Coconut water 1 liter

Cooking oil 2 tablespoons

Common seasoning 1 little

(sugar/salt/seasoning/monosodium glutamate)

Realization tools

Pressure cookers, blenders, pans, pots, scissors,...

How to cook Beef Noodles with an electric pressure cooker

1 Preliminary preparation and boiling of beef intestines

To remove the fishy smell and dirt, after buying, you use a razor to clean both sides, cut off the excess fat.

Then put the beef in a bowl with 100ml of vinegar, 1 tablespoon of salt and 1 tablespoon of baking soda, then squeeze and rub the beef intestines evenly for about 5 minutes, take out and rinse many times with water.

Small tip: Preliminary processing of beef intestines with vinegar and baking soda helps to make the intestines clean and whiter.

Put 2 liters of water in a pot and bring to a boil, then add to the pot 1 tablespoon salt, 2 slices of ginger, 1 onion cut into 4, 3 star anise, 1 tablespoon white wine, 2 tablespoons vinegar and bring the water to a boil again.

Next, add the beef intestines, cook for about 5 minutes, then remove the intestines, wash them 2-3 times with water and then drain.

Small tip: Boiling beef intestines with wine, vinegar, and anise helps to remove the fishy smell and after boiling, the beef intestines are white and beautiful, not darkened.

2 Prepare the marinade

Put in the blender 1 slice of ginger (about 3g), 3 cloves of garlic, 1 red onion, 1 teaspoon of five spice powder, 1.5 tablespoons of sugar, 3 tablespoons of soy sauce, 1 teaspoon of seasoning, 1 tablespoon salted coffee, a little dried chili, a little fresh chili, then cover and grind until the mixture is smooth.

Small tip: Depending on your taste and preference for spicy food, you can actively reduce the amount of chili accordingly!

3 Marinate beef intestines

Put the spice sauce mixture just ground into the beef, then mix and massage well. Marinate beef intestines for about 1 hour to infuse spices.

4 Stir-fry beef intestines

Heat a pan on the stove, add 2 tablespoons of cooking oil to heat, then add 3 crushed garlic cloves and 2 slices of ginger to fry until fragrant.

Next, put the beef intestines in and stir-fry the donkeys for about 5 minutes so that the intestines are hunted and fragrant, then take them out.

5 Behold the cow's heart

Put the beef in the pressure cooker, then add 1 liter of fresh coconut water.

Close the lid and lock the pot valve, select the Meat/Stew (Meat/Stew) cook button and cook on low (Less) for about 10 minutes.

After 10 minutes, you drain the valve, open the lid and mix the beef.

Continue to cover the lid, press the Sauté button and cook on the normal mode (Normal) for about 15 more minutes for the periwinkle, thickening and the beef intestines are soft.

Finally, add about 1/4 teaspoon of MSG, stir well and then turn off the heat.

6 Finished Products

Put the beef on a plate, use scissors to cut it into bite-sized pieces and then decorate it beautifully.

The dish of beef tripe with coconut milk has a beautiful yellow color with an attractive aroma. The chewy, lumpy beef intestine is seasoned to taste just right, stimulating the taste buds immensely.

This dish is served with hot rice or rice paper rolls, dipped with garlic soy sauce or sweet and sour fish sauce, all of which are wonderful!

BREAKING BEEF ZUCCHINI

Ingredients

Beef intestine 500 gr (including spleen/cane
leaves/honeycomb/potions)

Coconut milk 200 ml

Coconut water 1 liter

White wine 2 tablespoons

Garlic 2 bulbs

Minced purple onion 5 pieces

Ginger 1 piece

2 red chili peppers

Fish sauce 1 tablespoon

Juice of 1/2 tbsp

Cinnamon 1 pc

Anise flowers 2 pieces

Five flavors 1 teaspoon

Curry powder 1 teaspoon

Cooking oil 1 tablespoon

Common seasoning 1 little (salt/sugar/monosodium glutamate/seasoning/pepper)

Implementation tools:

Pressure cookers, bowls, stoves, pans, plates,...

How to cook Beef Broth with a pressure cooker

1 Preliminary processing of beef intestines

To clean the intestines, remove grease and odors, after buying, wash the intestines with a little alcohol and salt.

Then, take a pot of boiling water, add 1 tablespoon of salt and 1 crushed ginger root, put the leaves, honeycomb, and pho in turn until you see a scum (white foam), then take it out, put the sugar cane leaves in. Last blanching so that the other parts do not turn black, if the cane leaves are hard, then take them out.

Rinse the intestines with water to remove the oil and odor, and dry.

2 Marinate beef intestines

Put the intestines in a large bowl, add seasonings: 1/2 teaspoon curry powder, 1/2 teaspoon five spice powder and salt, sugar, seasoning seeds, monosodium glutamate, pepper, fish sauce, minced onion, minced garlic each 1 tablespoon in.

Mix well, marinate for 1 hour to absorb the spices.

3 Pre-fried beef intestines

Put the pan on the stove to high heat, add 1 tablespoon of cooking oil, hot oil for 1 minced garlic, 3 minced purple onions, 2 anise flowers, 1 cinnamon stick.

Put the intestines in and deep-fry for about 5 minutes, turning both sides until the heart is cooked evenly.

4 Making a pothole

Put the leaves, honeycomb, and Pheo into the pressure cooker, 1 liter of coconut water, and stew for 30 minutes.

After 30 minutes, put the sugarcane leaves into the stew for another 20 minutes, then pour 200ml of coconut milk in, season to taste, cook for about 5 more minutes.

5 Make kumquat fish sauce

Mix 2 tablespoons of sugar, 1/2 tablespoon of lime juice and 1 tablespoon of fish sauce, stir until the sugar dissolves. Add chili to taste.

CHICKEN STEW WITH GREEN BEANS

Ingredients

Chicken 2 kg (1 chicken)

Plain rice 100 gr

Green beans 100 gr

1 pinch salt

Implementation tools

Pressure cooker, cutting board, knife, basket, brass,...

How to cook Green Bean Stew Chicken

1 Preliminary processing of chicken

First, the chicken you bought, you proceed to blanch in boiling water and then use your hands to pluck the feathers away. After that, you just rinse with clean water a few times, and at the same time use your hands or tweezers to pull out the remaining hairs on the surface of the skin.

Next, remove all the dirty blood, intestines inside, cut off the legs and wings with a knife. Continue, rub a little salt on the surface of the chicken, then rinse with clean water a few times, then dry.

Pro tip: To save time, you can buy pre-cooked whole chicken!

How to prepare and deodorize chicken

Proceed to rub the meat with granulated salt and then wash it with water a few times so that the meat is clean and no longer foul.

Rub a mixture of crushed ginger and white wine on the chicken is also a very effective way to get rid of the smell.

Besides, you can use the way to soak the chicken in water with a little lemon juice, let it sit for about 15 minutes, then take it out, wash it again many times with clean water.

2 Wash green beans and put in

With plain rice and green beans, you proceed to wash it 1-2 times with water to remove all remaining dirt. Then, you put the whole rice and green beans inside the chicken!

3 Chicken stew

After preparing the ingredients, take the pressure cooker and add 1 chicken stuffed with green beans and 1.2 liters of water, cook with stew mode for 15-20 minutes.

When you see the chicken is cooked and the porridge has also hatched, turn off the heat, then put it in a bowl and enjoy!

4 Finished Products

Chicken stewed with hot green beans will be a delicious and attractive dish that no one can deny the attraction it brings.

Porridge is smooth, and still delicious because it is stewed with chicken, and then the chicken is firm, not greasy, another special thing is that it is green beans, which is fresh and delicious!

BEEF STEW TOMATO

Ingredients

Beef 900 gr

4 tomatoes

Green onion 1 branch

1/2 cup ginger

Pepper 1 teaspoon (whole grain)

Anise flowers 6 pieces

Dried laurel 3 leaves

Tomato paste 1 teaspoon (tomato paste)

White wine 1 tbsp

Soy sauce 1 tbsp

Black soy sauce 1/2 teaspoon

1 little coriander

Sugar/Salt 1 pinch

Cooking oil 1 tablespoon

Implementation tools

Pressure cooker, pot, knife, cutting board, bowl,...

How to cook Beef Stew with Tomato

1 Preliminary processing of ingredients

Wash the ginger with water, then slice it. Wash tomatoes, then use a knife to cut the areca.

Cut the scallions from the root, wash them, and then use a knife to cut them into pieces about 2 fingers long.

Prepare 1 cloth bag, put scallions, ginger, 3 bay leaves, 6 star anise, 1 teaspoon pepper and tie tightly.

2 Preliminary processing of beef

To remove dirt and odors, the beef you buy should be soaked with diluted salt water for about 5-10 minutes, then rinsed with cold water and drained.

Next, use a knife to cut the beef into bite-sized squares about 1.5 - 2 fingers thick.

Small tip: Do not cut beef too small, it will cause the beef to easily disintegrate while stewing.

How to remove the smell of beef:

Method 1: Soak beef in white wine for 15 minutes and then rinse with clean water.

Method 2: Put the beef in a pot of water, boil for about 3-5 minutes, then take it out and wash the meat to reduce the smell. Note that you only heat about 50 degrees Celsius, not boil.

Method 3: Use lemon or vinegar to rub on the beef for 5-7 minutes and then rinse with clean water.

Method 4: Bake 1 ginger root, then pound it, rub it on the beef and then wash it clean.

3 Boiled beef

Put the beef in the pot and pour the water to cover the meat. Put the pot on the stove and continue to cook over high heat until the water in the pot boils and foam appears.

Next, take out the beef, rinse it with water to remove the foam, and then let it dry.

4 Stir-fry beef

Heat the pressure cooker on "Sauté" for 3 - 5 minutes.

Next, add 1 tablespoon of cooking oil to heat, then add the beef and saute for about 2-3 minutes until the meat is tender and drained.

Next, add 1 teaspoon of tomato paste, 1 tablespoon of white wine, 1 tablespoon of soy sauce, 1/2 teaspoon of black soy sauce and stir for 3-5 minutes for the meat to absorb the spices.

Pro tip: Because tomato paste has a much stronger flavor than ketchup, you need to pay attention to the dosage to avoid making the dish too sour and pungent!

5 Beef stew with tomatoes
When the meat has absorbed the spices, you add the tomatoes and stir-fry for about 3 minutes until the tomatoes are just cooked.

Add 1 teaspoon of sugar and the prepared seasoning bag to the pot, add 120ml of filtered water (about 1 cup) and stir well.

Cover the pot, select "Meat/Stew" mode and proceed to stew meat for 30 minutes. After 30 minutes, you release the pressure valve and continue to incubate the beef in the pot for about 10 more minutes.

Next, you open the lid of the pot, take out the seasoning bag, then add 1/4 teaspoon of salt to the pot.

Switch the pressure cooker to "Sauté" mode and cook for another 3 minutes, then season to taste, then turn off the heat.

6 Complete

Scoop the tomato stewed beef into a bowl, add a little cilantro on top and then decorate it beautifully and you're done.

7 Finished Products

Beef stewed with tomato after being finished has a beautiful red color, with a passionate aroma of ginger, star anise, laurel and pepper. Stewed beef is soft, evenly absorbed with spices, mixed with the sweet and sour taste of tomatoes to create a sense of stimulating taste.

This dish you can use with white rice, bread or fresh vermicelli is extremely great!

BEEF WITH WINE SAUCE

Ingredients

Beef tenderloin 400 gr

Potatoes 300 gr (about 2 bulbs)

1 carrot

1 tomato

Onion 130 gr (about 1 bulb)

Cinnamon 2 branches

Ginger 1 bulb (small tuber)

Garlic 4 cloves

Red wine 30 ml

Tapioca powder 2 tablespoons

Cooking oil 3 tablespoons

Wine seasoning 5 gr

Common seasoning 1 little (monosodium glutamate / seasoning / salt / sugar / ground pepper)

Implementation tools

Pressure cookers, chopsticks, pans, knives, food wrap

How to cook Beef with Wine Sauce in a Pressure Cooker

1 Preliminary processing and marinating of beef

Buy beef to remove the smell, you wash the meat briefly with dilute salt water, then rinse 2-3 times with clean water, then drain and cut into bite-sized squares with a length of about 1.5 fingers.

How to prepare beef without smell

Method 1: Soak beef with vinegar for about 5 minutes, then rinse with clean water.

Method 2: Rub salt with beef, leave for 5 minutes and then rinse with water.

Method 3: Rub lemon on beef for about 3 minutes, then rinse with water before processing.

After washing the tomatoes, cut them into small pieces. Onions you peel, wash and cut areca

Garlic you peeled, smashed, chopped and divided into 2 equal parts. Ginger you peel, wash and chop finely.

Next, you put the square-cut beef into a bowl with 1 tablespoon MSG, 1 tablespoon seasoning powder, 1/2 tablespoon salt, 1 tablespoon sugar, 5g wine sauce seasoning (about 1 teaspoon), 1 /2 tbsp ground pepper, 1/2 minced garlic, minced ginger.

Then, use chopsticks to mix well and cover the mouth of the bowl with cling film and marinate for about 1 hour for the meat to absorb the seasoning.

2 Cook beef in wine sauce

Put the pan on the stove, add 3 tablespoons of cooking oil, wait until the oil is hot, add the remaining 1/2 of the minced garlic and fry until fragrant golden brown on high heat for about 20 seconds.

Then, add the marinated beef and stir-fry for about 2 minutes on high heat, then add 30ml of red wine and chopped tomatoes and stir-fry for another 2 minutes, then turn off the heat.

Next, you put the sautéed meat in the pressure cooker, 1/2 tablespoon of salt, add 2 cinnamon branches and 700ml of water. Cover and simmer for 20 minutes.

Finally, you release the valve to reduce the heat, wait for about 2 minutes, then open the lid to let the potatoes and carrots in.

Tapioca will help the dish become thicker and richer, so you dissolve 2 tablespoons of tapioca with 30ml of water in the pot and cover the stew for another 10 minutes to complete.

Note:

During the cooking process in the pressure cooker, you must not open the lid, even to taste.

When the stew is long enough, you can release the valve, then let it rest for about 2-3 minutes before opening the lid of the pot.

3 Finished Products

Once you're done, scoop out the beef into a bowl and serve hot with vermicelli, bread or hot rice

LAGU PORK LOIN

Ingredients

Pork sausage 800 gr

Carrots 2 pieces

Onion 1 piece

White beans 1 box (about 425g)

Cornstarch 2 tbsp (can be substituted with tapioca flour)

Green onion 2 branches

Coriander 2 branches

2 chili peppers

Purple onion 2 pieces

Satay 2 tbsp

Fish sauce 2 tablespoons

Cooking oil 2 tablespoons

Common seasoning 1 little (seasoning powder/sugar/pepper/salt)

Implementation tools

Pressure cooker, bowl, chopsticks, spoon, basket,...

How to make Lagu with pork rinds

1 Preliminary processing of pork shank
When you buy pork rolls, you wash them with water to remove dirt.

Put a pot of water on the stove to boil and put 1 teaspoon of salt in the pot, when the water boils, put the pork leg into the pot and blanch it for 3 minutes.

After 3 minutes, when you see that the pork leg is hunting again, take it out, wash it thoroughly with cold water to clean it, and then let it dry.

How to prepare clean, no-smell pork rolls

Method 1: Before processing into dishes, boil pork shank in boiling water for 2-3 minutes, then rinse with cold water.

Method 2: Use a mini gas torch to turn on medium mode or burn excess newspaper and straw to shrink the pig's thighs, thoroughly removing the hard hair on the surface of the pig's skin. However, you should use a mini gas torch because it is more convenient and easier to control the fire, to avoid burning the pork belly.

Method 3: Besides, you can use vinegar, wine or lemon juice to rub on the sides of the legs and the crevices to remove the fishy smell.

2 Preliminary preparation of other ingredients

The white beans are poured from the box and drained of the soaking water, washed in cold water to clean and remove the viscosity, and then drained.

When you buy carrots, cut off the stalks, peel them, wash them, and then cut them into small pieces.

Cut the onion root, peel and wash, then cut in half. Put the onions in a bowl of ice cold water to keep them from being pungent.

Coriander cut off the root, pick up the wilted slices, smother it, wash it, and dry it.

3 Marinate pork shank
Puree 2 chili peppers with 2 dried onions.

After being cleaned and dried, put the pork leg in a large bowl and marinate with 1 teaspoon of salt, 1 teaspoon of seasoning powder, 1 teaspoon of sugar, 1/2 teaspoon of pepper.

Add 2 tablespoons of fish sauce, 2 tablespoons of satay, and a mixture of crushed onions and chili peppers. Mix well until the seasoning is evenly spread over the whole pork leg.

Marinate pork leg for 30 minutes for the meat to absorb the spices.

4 Stew with pork shank

Put the pot on the stove over high heat and heat 2 tablespoons of oil. When the oil is boiling, add 2 crushed garlic cloves and fry until fragrant.

When the garlic has turned yellow and has a strong smell, add the marinated pork loin and stir-fry on high heat until the meat is hunted, then add 3 liters of filtered water and onions to the pot. Cover, reduce heat to medium and simmer for 60 minutes.

After stewing for 60 minutes, you open the lid of the pot to remove the onion,

In turn, add carrots and white beans to the stew for another 20 minutes.

5 Complete

Mix 2 tablespoons of cornstarch (or tapioca) in a cup with 4 tablespoons of filtered water, stir until the powder is dissolved and there are no lumps.

Slowly add the dissolved flour into the stewing pot, you can increase or decrease the amount of flour mixture so that the broth has a satisfactory consistency.

Seasoning for the last time to make the broth just right, the dish is done.

6 Finished Products

Lagu pork rolls is an easy dish to make but takes a long time to stew, but produces extremely delicious and attractive finished products.

After 90 minutes of stewing, the meat is soft, succulent with natural sweetness and evenly absorbed with spices, the skin is inside and flexible.

White beans and carrots are stewed soft, fatty and delicious. Lagu served with bread or vermicelli is delicious and delicious, suitable for every family menu.

GAC STICKY RICE

Materials to prepare:

Sticky rice

Ripe Gac

White wine

Salt

Cooking oil

Coconut

How to cook Gac sticky rice with a mechanical pressure cooker:

Step 1: Prepare ingredients

Soak glutinous rice (should choose the type of sticky rice with yellow flowers) overnight for about 6-8 hours so that when cooking, the rice grains are most flexible. After soaking, wash it clean, remove the grit and then drain.

Cut the ripe Gac fruit in half, use a ladle to remove all the intestines and put them in a separate bowl, add white wine to the Gac meat and squeeze to help the Gac become redder.

Next, mix Gac with rice, add a little white salt. Let it sit for about 10 minutes and then bring it to boil.

For Siamese coconut, we use a knife to cut out the water and separate the pulp. The pulp we will scrape into fibers to use with sticky rice after the sticky rice is cooked.

The coconut water we will put up to cook to cook coconut milk, then below the boiling part is cooking.

Step 2: Cook sticky rice with a pressure cooker

Put the steaming tray on the pot lined with banana leaves, at the bottom of the pot pour 1 amount of filtered water, depending on the rice we give more or less.

Pour the rice mixed with gac into the tray, cover the lid and start steaming. When steaming for 15 minutes, we pour coconut milk and a little cooking oil on top, then steam for another 10 minutes.

When sticky rice is cooked, you can mix in sugar to enjoy.

BONE BROTH

Ingredients for making bone broth

Pork bone 500 gr

Noodles 400 gr

2 stalks white cabbage

1 carrot

Green onion 1 piece

Coriander 1 little

Common seasoning 1 little (salt/monosodium glutamate/seasoning/pepper)

Implementation tools

Pressure cooker, brass, knife, cutting board,...

How to cook Boneless Noodles

1 Preliminary processing of ingredients

Buy pork bones, soak in diluted salt water for about 10 minutes, then rinse thoroughly with water, drain and marinate with 1 teaspoon of salt.

Tips for preparing pork bones not fishy:

Method 1: Purchased pork bones are washed, then blanched briefly in boiling water for about 2-3 minutes, then removed all bones, rinsed with clean water.

Method 2: Soak the washed pork bones with diluted salt water for about 25-30 minutes. When the time is up, take it out and rinse it under running water.

Method 3: In addition, ingredients such as dried onions, white wine, vinegar, ginger, lemongrass, ... also have the effect of eliminating the odor of pork bones, when blanching the bones, you can put these ingredients in.

White radish and carrot are peeled, washed and cut into round slices to taste.

Put the noodles in a bowl, soak them in hot water for about 20 minutes, then boil them for 5-7 minutes, then rinse them with cold water to keep them from clumping.

2 Cook noodles

Put the bones, carrots, and white radish in the pot, add water up to the highest mark and select the soup mode.

When cooking is finished, the light flashes, then you let the steam out and open the pressure lid and then switch to the 2nd level hot pot cooking mode.

When finished cooking in hot pot mode, add a spice mixture including: 1 teaspoon salt, 1 teaspoon MSG, 2 tablespoons seasoning. Then you cook for about 3 more minutes and then turn off the stove.

3 Finished Products

Put the broth in a bowl with noodles, sprinkle a little more pepper, scallions, and cilantro, and you're done.

The noodle bowl has an attractive color thanks to a variety of ingredients. Soft and chewy noodles combined with sweet broth, rich meat and bones ensure that anyone who eats will be addicted to it.

SAUSAGE LEG STEW WITH LOTUS SEEDS

Materials to prepare:

1 whole pork leg (should choose the front leg to eat better)

Lotus seeds

Carrot

Onion

Mushrooms

Commonly used spices

How to make stewed pork leg with lotus seeds using an electric pressure cooker:

Step 1: Prepare ingredients

Buy pork leg to shave off the hair, peel off the nails, wash it, cut it into bite-sized pieces. Then marinate the pork leg with pepper, seasoning powder, 1 tablespoon fish sauce and then put it in the refrigerator for about 2 hours to infuse the spices.

Lotus seeds, shiitake mushrooms soaked to bloom. Onions, remove the stem, wash, dry and cut into wedges. Carrots are peeled, washed and cut into pieces.

Step 2: Stew pork feet with lotus seeds

Marinate lotus seeds first and set aside.

After marinating the pork leg, bring it into the pot and pour about 2/3 of the pot of water to cook. Plug in the power, set the time about 15 minutes. Then, quickly release the steam to open the pot, then add lotus seeds, carrots, and onions and wait for another 5 minutes to finish.

BRAISED DUCK ALLIGATOR

Materials needed:

Duck meat is cleaned

Green Crocodile

Lemongrass, ginger, garlic, green onion

cilantro

The smell of ships

Cooking oil

Fish sauce

Common condiments

How to make braised duck with an electric pressure cooker:

Clean duck, cut into bite-sized pieces. Lemongrass cut the root, wash, cut the head of lemongrass thinly, the tail of lemongrass is smashed. Peel the ginger, wash it and cut it into small pieces. Wash and dry the scallops.

You bring the garlic peeled and minced, scallions and coriander, cut the root, wash and then cut into small pieces.

Marinate duck meat with salt, ginger, sliced lemongrass, sugar, 1 tablespoon cooking oil for about 30 minutes. After marinating, put a little oil in the pot, select the high heat pan and sauté the meat until it's tender.

Next, add in the batter, stir-fry for about 3 more minutes, then put half a liter of coconut water in the pot, then close the lid, select the high pressure cooking mode for 15 minutes.

At the end of 15 minutes, quickly release the steam, open the pot, add scallions, and the smell of the boat, stir for another 2 minutes. Finally unplug the stove, scoop the finished food into a large bowl.

CHICKEN SOUP

Materials to prepare:

1 chicken

Rice 700g

Lemongrass, ginger, green onion

Common condiments

How to cook chicken porridge with an electric pressure cooker:

Wash the rice clean, then soak for about 1 hour so that the rice grains are soft, when cooked quickly expand and absorb more flavor. Wash the chicken, cut it into pieces, filter the skin, keep only the skin on the chicken wings.

Next, put about half a liter of water in the pressure cooker, add the rice, set the "Sauté" mode to "More" to heat the water in the pot first. When white foam emerges, take it out. Turn on this mode when cooking porridge, there is no need to cover the lid.

When the porridge starts to boil, the porridge seeds expand, then add the chicken, smash the discharge and add the ginger. Add a little salt, seasoning, and sugar to taste, then stir gently.

After that, you press the "Cancel" button, then close the pot lid, lock the valve and switch to "Porridge" mode at "Normal" and timer for about 8-10 minutes to complete. You can sprinkle a little more pepper, scallions into the bowl of porridge to enjoy.

CHICKEN COOKED WITH SHIITAKE MUSHROOMS STEWED

Ingredients

Chicken thighs 8 pieces

Shiitake mushrooms 100 gr (dry)

Draft beer 330 ml (1 can)

Purple onion 1 piece

Garlic 4 cloves

Ginger 1 branch

Green onion 1 piece

Red Chao 2 pieces

Soy sauce 2 tablespoons

Oyster oil 1 tbsp

Common seasoning 1 pinch (salt/sugar/pepper)

How to cook Chicken cooked with shiitake mushrooms

1 Preliminary processing of chicken

When you buy chicken thighs, you pull out the fluff (if any), to remove the smell of chicken, take the chicken thighs and soak them in warm water for about 20 minutes. Then rinse with clean water and dry.

Small tip: In addition, you can eliminate the odor of chicken by the following.

Mix a mixture of salt and vinegar in a ratio of 1:2 and then apply it all over the chicken several times, then rinse with clean water.

You can replace vinegar with ginger or lemon in the recipe above.

To make chicken thighs easier to absorb spices when marinating, use a bamboo toothpick (or fork) to poke small holes on the chicken thigh.

2 Preliminary preparation of other ingredients
Buy dried shiitake mushrooms and soak them in warm water for about 20 minutes to help soften them, then wash them with clean water and squeeze them out.

Red onion, garlic you peel and slice thinly. Peel the ginger and cut it into thin slices.
Green onions you cut off the roots and yellow leaves, wash and dry, then cut into small pieces.

3 Marinated chicken
Put all the chicken thighs in a bowl and season with the seasoning mixture including: 2 pieces of red colander, 2 tablespoons soy sauce, 1 tablespoon oyster sauce, 1 teaspoon pepper, 1 teaspoon salt, 1 teaspoon sugar.

Then mix well and marinate for 30 minutes to allow the chicken thighs to absorb the spices.

4 Chicken stew

Put all the sliced shallots, garlic, and ginger in the pressure cooker, then put the whole marinated chicken thighs into the pot.

Next, you pour into 1 can of beer and top with all the dried shiitake mushrooms that have been soaked. Close the lid and simmer the chicken over medium heat for about 15 minutes.

After 15 minutes, you open the lid of the pot, stir the ingredients and cook for another 5 minutes, you can turn off the stove. Scoop the chicken cooked with shiitake mushrooms and stew with fresh beer in a bowl, sprinkle some chopped scallions on top and enjoy immediately.

Pro tip: If you use a regular pot or a rice cooker to cook the chicken, increase the time to about 25 minutes for the chicken to be tender.

5 Finished Products

Chicken cooked with shiitake mushrooms stewed with fresh beer is not too difficult to complete, right? The tender chicken is imbued with the flavor of soy sauce, oyster sauce and especially the aroma of fresh beer, dried shiitake mushrooms, crispy and crunchy.

There's nothing better than eating with white rice or bread. Come to the kitchen to show off your family skills on days when everyone is tired of eating meat and fish.

CONTENTS

Printed in Great Britain
by Amazon